The I

Homestead

Learn True Sustainability at Home, Off
Grid Green Living, Self-Reliance, Urban
Gardening plus Backyard Homesteading
Techniques

Be self-sufficient no matter where you
live!

By

Sara Manchester

Autumn Leaf
Publishers

Design & Illustration by Susan Kennedy

First Edition

Contents

Special Thanks

I would first like to thank you, the reader of this book. I love that you are interested in what I am so passionate about – saving the Earth while saving ourselves through sustainable living, self-reliance, and going green. You and I are modern homesteaders.

I would also like to extend a heartfelt thanks to my grandparents. As you'll see in the introduction, they gave me my first taste of what the dirt could yield with hard work and determination. Thank you, Mee-maw and Pop-pop!

Finally, I dedicate this book to the generations who will inherit the Earth. Let us leave it to them in a better condition than when we came upon it.

Introduction

I will never forget all those summers spent running around my grandparents' farm. The heat was relentless, but the days were bright, and it was during those days when I found just how much nature mattered to me. I fell in love with everything, from the sights and sounds of the farm to the quiet pride of the flowers and the plants, all coming together in this self-sustained agriculture of both flora and fauna.

It was my grandparents' smiles that mattered most of all. It wasn't all just sunshine and butterflies, gathering around the table to partake of that week's harvest amid organic produce and the freshest and choicest of meats. The backbreaking work came with it—they had spent forever tilling and farming and making sure all that nature had placed under their care received the love they deserved. It was then that things dawned on me with clarity and conviction—it was hard work, but at the end of the day, it was all about love, too.

I suppose it was those younger years that shaped the way I thought about nature as I grew up. I always knew that saving the planet should be on everyone's top priority list, but realistically speaking, how can you make a difference in such a great big world? It's the most daunting task anyone can ever take on, and it's not the least bit easy to do. I also knew that I couldn't very well just build a farm of my own, not when I'm living in the suburbs amid bustling civilization, with a job and a family and responsibilities I need to face.

But the Herculean task doesn't have to be grand and earth-shattering. At first, I thought I could just start small—plant a few veggies from scraps, maybe tend to a little hanging potted garden in the kitchen, and check up on some makeshift pots near the windowsill. But the moment the very first leaves sprouted from my bok choy scraps, I was hooked—and the rest, as they say, is history.

Today, my backyard is a self-sustained ecosystem of its own, the permaculture very much alive and thriving, helping me and my family live the truly self-reliant life. It wasn't the easiest and quickest road getting here, but all the troubles that came with DIY bushcraft were all worth it in the end. You don't need to go permanently off the grid to enjoy living off the land—all it takes is a little bit of patience, a chockfull of know-how, and a huge heaping of love. The love and patience are all up to you, but as for the knowledge part, I can definitely help you with that! This book will give you a running start to beginning your own modern homestead today.

If you have the means to be able to set out on your own on a large piece of property as my grandparents did, then I wish you the best. This book can help you get started. The majority of us will have to stick to working a daily nine-to-five job and make the most of our little quarter-acre lot in suburbia. Even with leading a traditional work life/home life lifestyle with a 3 bedroom house and 2.5 kids, we can develop habits that will better pass the Earth to the next generation.

Even more of us live in urban environments. However, in a city, you can still live a modern, self-sustainable, green lifestyle. There are little things that you can do that will help you save resources, including time and money.

No matter what part of the self-reliant spectrum you fall on, there are tips, tricks, and techniques you can employ to help you reach your goals. From fully off-grid country-style life to urban balcony gardening, you can help yourself and the environment (and be better prepared to deal with any crisis that your family may face because you rely on yourself and not the food supply chain!).

I. Sustainable Living

You've heard it all before, from big, bold, larger-than-life, and in-your-face billboard ads to small, quiet moments with a friend or two during those late-night talks. Sustainable living has always been a thing, but it should never just be a trend. It should be part of everyone's to-do list, and it encompasses everything we do, from the food that we eat to the way we live our life.

While you might be interested in starting a sustainable life, you might think it's impossible to leave all the comforts of technology and society behind. The good news is that sustainable living doesn't have to be that way. You can have a self-reliant and sustainable lifestyle by providing for yourself while still maintaining your jobs and staying close to your family and friends. Yes, you can still continue living in your own neighborhood—all that you need to do is to rely on stores and supply chains as little as possible.

Not everyone will have access to a natural pond or solar power every day. Still, sustainable living is actually easier than you might think!

A. What Is Sustainable Living?

You don't have to be Captain Planet to promote sustainable living. Sure, it affects everything we do—how we work, how we live, how we travel, and how we eat. But sustainable living can be done with simple, practical, down-to-earth, bite-sized, and realistic tasks that you can easily accomplish every day.

For instance, you know that you always get tons and tons of emails and ads about product updates that tempt you with new catalogs and the latest designs of apparel. You may even be receiving random junk mail, adding to the growing wastage of paper and natural resources that are used up and discarded year after year. You may not have signed up for these newsletters and junk mail on purpose (yes, we all know how annoying accidental sign-ups can be). Still, you CAN do something to stop those letters from coming. Simply unsubscribe from them!

Unsubscribing not only reduces your own carbon footprint simply by reducing all of that paper waste, but it also helps you refrain from buying things you don't really need. How many times have you been tempted to get the latest new fall collection or grab the latest gadget just because you found yourself enticed by things that ads show you? You may find excuses to buy new things—like the fact that your old ones are no longer working, or maybe you need the so-and-so feature to be more productive and efficient at work. But think about this—if you didn't see that ad in the first place, would you even have considered buying the newest model?

Aside from reducing your own contribution to consumerism, you can also do something as simple as knowing how much water you need to boil and drink with every serving. Not overboiling water in the kettle can already cut down your energy usage by a significant amount. These small steps can already help you live a more sustainable life without you even realizing it!

Basically, sustainable living means reducing your own demand on the resources of the environment. And if you do use up natural resources, it means that you are doing your very best to replace whatever you used and give back. This can also mean refusing to use a certain product because of manufacturing processes that do not encourage sustainability. You can also choose to play a more active part by helping with causes that promote lifestyle-altering movements against global warming, climate change, resource depletion, and the depletion of the ozone layer.

B. Sustainable Living Vs. Zero Waste — What's the Difference?

While both very similar in terms of lifestyle patterns, sustainable living, and zero waste can be very different things. Living sustainably means that you are reducing your overall impact on the environment and on natural resources. You can achieve this goal in a variety of different ways. With a zero-waste lifestyle, you are primarily focused on lowering the amount of trash—normally single-use plastic—that you produce daily.

The zero-waste movement may prompt someone to be okay with consuming meat products as long as they don't come in plastic packages. However, someone who is strictly following a more sustainable lifestyle may refuse to consume the meat product because of its overall impact on the environment. He or she may even further that goal by eliminating meat-based diets altogether for a more well-rounded and bigger picture of sustainability, especially when it comes to animal agriculture.

Your lifestyle will vary depending on how far you want to go with your sustainable lifestyle. However, regardless of how you approach the matter, all of these things still contribute to conserving natural resources, and ultimately saving Mother Earth.

C. How to Start Sustainable Living

There are so many wonderful ways you can start living sustainably—and you don't even have to go far to radically change your life! For instance, you can start easing yourself into a purely plant-based diet—this means that you will be lowering your impact on Mother Earth by reducing your consumption of meat, dairy, and eggs. You can transition into more vegan meals, or simply minimize food wastage whenever you eat or prep meals.

When it comes to composting, you can use food scraps like avocado pits, vegetable peels, and spoiled leftovers and use them as biodegradable elements to return them to the soil. Instead of sending them over to the landfill, you can use this composting technique by setting up a compost bin in your backyard—as simple as that!

Another way you can live sustainably is to take a page out of the zero waste movement's book—reduce your reliance on single-use plastic. Look through your trash and check to see how much single-use plastic you're consuming every day— you just might be surprised! Instead of clogging your garbage with single-use plastics, use plastic-free alternatives. Try to look for reusable alternatives to whatever you're using, whether it's a personal hygiene product or a disposable container.

Perhaps one of the most impactful and significant ways you can try to live sustainably is to evaluate the way you travel every day. Whenever you step out of the house, how do you make use of transportation options around you? Do you drive a gas-powered car daily? If you have the chance to lower your emissions, do so—you can ride a bike (that's good exercise, too!), walk, take the public transportation system, or carpool. If you really need to drive, research electric or hybrid alternatives to reduce your carbon footprint.

Aside from refraining from using plastic bags whenever you're shopping, you can also make it a habit to shop second-hand when you can. If you can check whether or not your favorite brand follows sustainable practices when manufacturing, by all means, do so! Just remember to have enough conviction for refusing when you find something that doesn't fit your new sustainable lifestyle—and be brave about it!

D. Why Is Sustainable Living Important?

Haven't you ever felt the unbearable heat on your back and the sweat on your brow, even when the weather isn't even supposed to be that hot? Climate change and global warming issues are growing more and more alarming each day. While it can be overwhelming, we can actually do something about it before it's too late.

Doing your part is now more important than ever. Your own impact can actually make a big difference, even if you might not think so in the beginning. On average, a regular American will produce 4.4 pounds of trash every single day, which is why if even just a single person decides to live a more sustainable lifestyle, it will already greatly impact the environment in so many ways and help reduce greenhouse gas emissions.

With your new lifestyle change, you can help reduce the usage of resources and fossil fuels. These fossil fuels then won't be able to release carbon into the earth's atmosphere and will then reduce the number of rising temperatures across the globe. Who would have thought that slowing down global warning could be this easy?

Now, while living sustainably might seem like an expensive lifestyle choice, there are many ways you can reduce your carbon footprint without spending a huge chunk of your savings—and that's exactly what we'll talk about in the rest of this book!

Aside from the impact of sustainable living on the world we live in today, reducing your carbon footprint will also ensure a better future for our children and future generations. You can help combat poverty, mitigate climate change, and help clean up Mother Earth just by choosing to live a sustainable lifestyle day by day.

If you want to make an impact and fight the growing rate of poverty, inequality, and discrimination among children, you have to do your part in furthering sustainable development because environmental degradation impacts children more. Floods, extreme weather conditions, and natural disasters bring more impoverished children to the streets, destroying homes and orphaning them with every occasion. Aside from issues on hunger, not everyone will have access to clean water and good air quality.

By practicing sustainable living, you can help conserve earth's natural resources so that the future generation will thrive. Commitment to this kind of lifestyle may not be easy at first. Still, if you try to learn how to live sustainably and self-reliantly day by day, you'll eventually get the hang of it!

E. The Three Pillars of Sustainability

According to the World Summit on Social Development in 2005, there are three core areas where you can focus on to contribute to sustainable development in terms of social sciences and philosophy. Along with certification schemes, national standards, and creating the backbone of social development, these pillars will help meet the needs of individuals during the present time without compromising the demands of living for future generations. With these conscious decisions that we make in the present, we can help save the future as well.

What does sustainability hope to achieve in the first place? This is a global goal that should address the end of poverty and hunger, ideally. It hopes to provide improvements in the standards of excellence when it comes to healthcare, such as better water quality and more humane standards of sanitation. It aims to increase levels of education, achieve gender equality, and contribute to overall economic growth. It should be able to further stronger commercial systems, as well as promote better jobs.

All of these may seem like lofty ideals. Still, sustainable development isn't all about caring for nature—it's a tightly interconnected web, or a chain reaction, of a variety of industries and aspects of living. Who would have thought that by just getting rid of single-use plastics, you can help do your part to make this world a better place, now and in all the years to come?

Sustainability also includes facing the issues of climate change and pollution head-on. It hopes to eliminate various environmental factors that are harmful to the livelihoods and overall well-being of people, as well as ensuring the health conditions of life on land, in the air, and under the sea.

More importantly, it also acknowledges the rights of nature. Human beings may have stewardship over the rest of the world, but that also means we are in charge of taking care of the resources in the environment. This includes proper management of nature and fair consumption, such as discouraging the use of harmful packaging, promoting recyclable materials, and reducing unnecessary waste.

1. Economic Development

The first pillar of sustainable development affects businesses, both big and small. It impacts jobs and employability, as sustainable development means that companies must strictly adhere to the guidelines of sustainability. It should also provide incentives for individuals to do their part when they can. It's important for people to understand that everything they do can have big impacts on the world as a whole.

Modern life imposes demands on natural resources every day. What we consume today greatly affects what the future generation will be able to consume in the years to come. As such, companies, governments, and other organizations and educational institutions should make sustainable practices as easy and hassle-free as possible, reducing any red tape from legislation whenever possible.

2. Social Development

Perhaps the most important aspect of social development when it comes to sustainability is the facet of awareness. People should be aware of the social impact of protecting healthcare as a whole. There must also be strong checks and balances that keep companies and organizations all over the world in line when it comes to exploiting natural resources. These programs must be strongly protected so as not to compromise the quality of life of individuals and social groups.

For instance, how can we promote sustainable housing? How can we create homes from more sustainable materials? How can we live a self-reliant life, and how can we reduce how much we take from the environment every day?

More importantly, how can we educate people to act as a cohesive society in living more sustainable lives? Teaching people about the effects of sustainable living and the ins and outs of environmental protection is important, because if people don't know what they're doing wrong, how can they correct them?

3. Environmental Protection

Finally, environmental protection is at the core of sustainable development. We need to protect the environment to make sure that the way we live now will be sustained for future generations to come.

There are many ways we can do just that! Recycling, reducing power consumption every day, switching off devices that consume power instead of leaving electronic devices on standby, walking instead of driving, and keeping carbon emissions as low as possible are just some of the ways you can help each day.

For businesses, there can be various incentives in place if they stick to renewable energy sources. If you install renewable power sources inside your home, you can not only save up on your electricity bill, but you can also reduce your overall demand on the environment. This will already provide you with an edge when it comes to protecting ecosystems, keeping the air quality high, and reducing the stress that humans place on the environment.

F. A Sustainable Future

With all of these important steps, we can take, starting your journey to sustainable living should be a no-brainer! Humanity is truly progressing with emerging technologies that eliminate harmful fuel sources. We are continuously trying to find better ways to use cleaner energy. There has been an unprecedented growth in these aspects, but of course, it's still not enough.

We all need to do our part—which is why I wrote this book for you. Living off the land is fun, rewarding, and environment friendly. Yes, you have it in you to preserve Mother Earth as much as you can. You can easily become an eco-warrior with just a little bit of patience and a whole lotta heart.

II. The History of Homesteading

Just where did all of this start in the first place? We hear about sustainable living and sustainable development all the time—but have we always been this conscious about it, and how did all the fuss about sustainability begin?

A. History of Sustainability

Even during the Neolithic Agricultural Revolution, human beings have always been more of consumers rather than replenishers. Societies have always taken a more hunter-gatherer approach since the beginning of time, and settlements were chosen based on how well a certain area can naturally provide for man's needs. Constant pressure on the environment has always been a given.

The growing human population further increased the harsh demands on the environment as time went on. Even permanent settlements eventually had to relocate to better and "greener" pastures when the environment in their current locations could no longer sustain their lives. Sustainable living didn't really matter back then, as exhausted resources could easily be replaced, improved upon using technology, or abandoned and left to find somewhere better elsewhere.

Of course, societies inevitably collapsed due to not being able to adapt to limited resources. Unsustainable practices such as cutting down trees at a faster rate than we can plant them can easily upset the balance of nature, destroying any semblance of sustainability in the ecosystem. Even humans were soon unable to adapt to the sudden and harsh changes in the atmosphere, such as fluctuations in weather and climate.

Today, we are becoming more and more aware of the damage we are causing to the environment thanks to the modernity of our world. Overpopulation is also a key issue, as the more people demand more from the world, the more pressure and stress we impose upon limited resources.

When the United Nations was founded in 1945 after World War II, part of its goals was to help cultivate the importance of sustainable development.

UNESCO was established, and it continues to further intercultural dialogue across cultures and sciences to help combat climate change and the greenhouse effect among others today.

Perhaps the birth of the movement to deter the destruction of the ozone layer might not have come as early as we would have wanted. Still, it's better to be late than never, which is why homesteading is becoming more and more popular as people all over the world strive to live self-reliant lives by living off the land and going off the grid. But how exactly did homesteading come to be?

B. Homestead Act

The Homestead Act of 1862 essentially let Americans put in claims of federal land. This helped facilitate the settlement of U.S. western territory. The petition can be put in for up to 160 acres for free.

President Abraham Lincoln signed the act on the 20th of May. The price was only for a minimal filing fee—this was in line with Lincoln's speech on July 4, 1861, where he said that the government should be able "to elevate the condition of men, to lift artificial burdens from all shoulders and to give everyone an unfettered start and a fair chance in the race of life."

Because of the Homestead Act, 10 percent or 270 million acres of U.S. land was claimed. There was only a filing fee of $18, provided that settlers had to live there for five years of continuous residence. People would build their homes there and farm the land to make improvements, as necessary.

The act came with its own set of problems (fraud and false claims included). Still, perhaps it was what truly spearheaded how people took care of their own lands and cultivated them in order to live self-sustained lives.

C. The Victory Gardens

At the height of World War I, there was a severe food crisis that swept Europe mainly because the agricultural workers who tilled the land were recruited into the military. Farms, instead of being tended to and cultivated, became battlegrounds for military service. The United States had to step up and take responsibility for feeding the millions who were starving.

The National War Garden Commission was then established in March 1917 by Charles Lathrop Pack. This aimed to promote the American people's contribution to the war by planting their own produce. This also included fertilizing, harvesting, and storing food to export to allies in the war. It transformed all idle lands like schools, parks, company grounds, and backyards into agricultural mini-farms for agricultural production.

"Sow the seeds of victory" was the slogan for citizens to be encouraged to plant their own fruits and vegetables. This movement spread across the country, as pamphlets were provided for amateur gardeners in order to teach the public how to sow, when and where to do so, and how to use best practices on maximizing the land's produce. The movement also taught people how to prevent diseases and keep insect infestations at bay.

When the results came in and turned out to be more favorable than expected, the government went on to spread awareness on canning, drying, and preserving surplus crops. The federal Bureau of Education also began the U.S. School Garden Army (USSGA), enlisting children to be "soldiers of the soil."

In the end, approximately 3 million new garden plots were created. The end of the First World War led to these "victory gardens," which remerged again during the Second World War. During this time, people became even more creative in their agricultural endeavors, planting mini-farms wherever there was any space—apartment rooftops, deserted parking lots, backyards, and small flower boxes included.

Produce planted included carrots, cabbages, beans, beets, Swiss chard, turnips, kohlrabi, tomatoes, turnips, lettuce, peas, and squash. People maximized productivity even further with more pamphlets. The Victory Garden campaign was incredibly effective not only in providing for the hungry but also in boosting overall morale during the war.

By 1944, there were approximately 20 million victory gardens created. The war may be long over, but the idea of self-sufficiency certainly stayed—now, people are more concerned about sustainable living, permaculture, and bushcraft more than ever.

D. The Great Depression

Perhaps another catalyst that inspired people to go into permaculture today is the worst economic crash in modern history. The Great Depression is aptly called such, as it affected how many American families lived their lives no matter what their social and economic statuses were.

From 1929 to 1939, the Great Depression forced many families to tighten their belts. Due in part to the stock market crash, many people lost their jobs—about a quarter of the workforce became unemployed.

Even those who weren't laid off experienced big pay cuts and reductions in their work hours. All of a sudden, families who once had economic security were faced with the harsh reality of financial instability.

Perhaps nothing describes the era more than the average American family's motto: "Use it up, wear it out, make do or do without." There were new levels of extreme frugality in every household, and as such, people started creating kitchen gardens and patching clothes that were worn-out. Thrift gardens became the norm, and people began to stretch out their budget for food and other resources via one-pot meals and other casseroles.

Among other ways to cope with the struggling economy was to practice self-sufficiency. Small kitchen gardens provided families with herbs and vegetables, while vacant lots were converted into thrift gardens so that residents of towns and cities can grow their own food.

For instance, the thrift garden program in Detroit was able to provide provisions for approximately 20,000 residents between 1931 and 1932.

E. Lessons Learned

Thankfully, humankind was able to get through the Great Depression in one piece, but that doesn't mean we came out unscathed. The hard times bring good lessons as they always do, and we need to keep them in mind to better improve ourselves and our lifestyles in all the years to come.

1. Don't be wasteful.

If you can, use your items more than once. During the Great Depression, people didn't have the luxury of using disposable items. Everything that might have been scrapped was reused and recycled, from cloth pieces to packaging.

Today, remember not to spend too much of your hard-earned money on something that you'll only be using once. The same is true with food—don't waste anything.

The Great Depression meant that people had to feed as many mouths as possible with few resources, so even the smallest portion of food had to be conserved.

2. Don't keep buying new stuff.

At the same time, don't open a new package of food until you've already finished the old one. This will help prevent any spoilage and will reduce your food wastes as well. This will also train you to be conscious of whatever you're buying—after all, you wouldn't buy a new pack of food if you know you're still finishing up the old one.

You can also use the same concept not just with food but with appliances and other gadgets as well. Sustainable living isn't just about organic materials—it also means conserving the use of energy and manufactured materials to reduce your overall carbon emissions. Yes, while it's tempting to grab the latest model of that smartphone or the newest vacuum cleaner with all the bells and whistles, remember that your old one is still working perfectly fine—you wouldn't keep buying new things if you were living during the Depression-era, would you?

3. Learn how to DIY.

Self-sustained lifestyles will help you learn how to do things yourself! This will not only reduce your reliance on outside supplies, but it will also help you be more resourceful whenever a new problem crops up. When something broke down, think about how people from the Depression-era didn't have the luxury to call someone up and have their equipment fixed. They also couldn't afford to buy new things to replace broken ones.

These days, it can be so easy to discard things with our modern consumerism and wasteful lifestyle. But if you learn to learn from the Great Depression, you can train yourself to be more resourceful. Does your jacket have holes on the sleeves? Why not revamp your clothing items into something else, like a shirt or a sweater you can sleep in? Why not re-create tattered clothes into rugs and mats?

Whenever you consume your veggies, don't throw out the stems! Plenty of plants can be grown from scraps with just a little bit of water, some sunlight, and a lot of TLC. You can also reuse packaging instead of throwing them out immediately. For instance, you can use old egg cartons as your base for growing a variety of herbs and veggies! Eggshells themselves are a good source of fertilizer when you break them down and scatter them across the soil.

You can repurpose old things into new things with just a little bit of patience and a lot of imagination. Pringles cans can be used as ornaments, and dirty mason jars can be used as holders for candles and other garden décor. All kinds of boxes can be used as stands, holders, and re-imagined containers. You can even use your old soda plastic bottles as containers for hanging vertical gardens—the possibilities are endless! You can DIY minor issues at home, and at the same time, you can even DIY your own veggie and herb garden—which is what we'll get right into in this book.

III. Why You Should (or Shouldn't) Go Self-Reliant

Living off the land is a brave decision—and a life-altering one. Now that you've decided to be self-reliant in your quest to live a more sustainable life, you have to be prepared for big changes in your day-to-day operations!

It's not as easy as waking up one day and realizing you want to go off the grid. While it's a big life change, it's also a fun and immensely rewarding one—but before you decide for good, let's look at the pros and cons of this kind of lifestyle so that you can make an informed decision and see if it's the best choice for you.

A. Pros

Are you tenacious, resilient, and a determined go-getter? Are you eager to solve problems? Are you gung-ho and upbeat when it comes to the great outdoors, and are you unafraid to get your hands dirty?

If you don't mind the occasional callous or cut, you just might be a good fit for the self-sufficient life. But living off the grid is easier said than done, and you have to be physically and mentally prepared for the plethora of issues you need to face once you actually get started. You not only have to know what you're doing (don't worry—I can help you with that!), but you also have to be stubborn when it comes to not giving up easily.

Living off the land, thriving, and actually surviving is hard work. But the thing about hopping right into the wonderful world of homesteading is that it also opens you up to a world of benefits you otherwise wouldn't have known if you never decided to be self-sufficient.

In itself, being self-sufficient means you will be relying mainly on yourself and your own resources, which is a benefit in itself. You grow your own food and raise your own meat, and you harvest energy from natural resources like it's nobody's business. Should outside sources like economies, supply chains, economies, and societies collapse, you'll still do fine on your own.

Being a permaculture pro also means that you will be living a more eco-friendly life. When you ditch the grid, you not only do your part in saving Mother Nature, but you also contribute to securing a good future for the next generation. There's an immense sense of satisfaction knowing that you are living your short journey in the world, not just for yourself but also for others. Bidding goodbye to the throwaway culture in favor of a more sustainable one is a rewarding feeling—one that you definitely can't find elsewhere.

When you live a sustainable living, you will also find that your costs diminish over time. Initially, you will be spending a lot of hard-earned cash to get everything up and running.

Start-up costs are always on the heavy side, but the burdens on your wallet will slowly start to ease up as you get used to everything and hit your stride. After all, once you've set up your home, tilled the soil, set up your power, and invested in your permaculture and bushcraft, you'll soon reap all of the benefits of your hard work (and your wallet will thank you for it). You will no longer have to pay exorbitant costs for hefty price tags associated with food and general consumption—plus, your own self-reliant set-up will last for a longer duration than the more temporary things you can buy outside.

Finally, living off the grid will also bring you closer to nature. You will be spending most of your time in the great outdoors, soaking up the sun and immersing yourself in all that nature has to offer—and there's nothing more fulfilling than that.

B. Cons

Of course, not everything is sunshine and butterflies when you're living off the grid. As mentioned, you will have big initial costs as you're setting up. It's definitely not cheap to start your own ecosystem per se. In essence, you're starting your own supply chain in hopes of living sustainably for years and years to come, so costs will inevitably be on the heavy side.

You will need to spend a lot on construction, water systems, power, supplies and equipment, and the actual acquisition of land itself if you don't have one yet. You also need to spend for heavy-duty equivalents of your normal everyday tools, as they will be bearing the brunt of the great outdoors 24/7, 365 days a year. Outdoor environments are more demanding, which is why all of your equipment must be able to withstand extreme weather conditions all year. Even a simple oversight—or trying to cut corners—can spell the difference between success and failure for your permaculture.

Staying off the grid will also bring the occasional loneliness every now and then. While you may not be distancing yourself completely or cutting yourself off from family and friends absolutely, you still won't be able to immerse yourself in your old society as much as you used to. Unless you're looking to live in a sort of communal environment, off-gridders will likely be feeling a little blue every so often.

You also have to give up a lot of modern conveniences when you're living off the land. Just think—if you're craving for a big, juicy, unhealthy burger in the middle of the night or it's just one of those days when a greasy pizza is an ideal solution to all of your problems, you can't just up and order from your favorite fast food joint. You will need to compromise a great deal more than just regular modern luxuries. You will have limited access to many things and many places, and you have to be able to give up these conveniences when you're off the grid.

Also, here's the thing—living off the land means you need to deal with all of the unpleasant smells that come with self-reliant living. No, I'm not even kidding! You really have to have a strong gut and a hardened sense of smell to be able to stomach all of the various smells and scents wafting in from outdoors. This is especially true if you have your own livestock. Manure isn't the only thing you have to look out for—even if you're just planting veggies, there will still be smells from the soil, the plants, rotting flora, and pests or bugs buzzing about.

If you have a more sensitive sense of smell, it can be hard to stomach the natural smells that come with self-reliant living. No matter how hard you try to mask the smell with various artificial scents indoors, eventually, everything will start to smell the same way—from your personal items down to your clothes! It definitely takes some getting used to.

Finally, homesteading requires effort—and I mean a lot of effort. It takes time to get used to everything, and it takes a great deal of patience to be able to get everything up and running. You really have to commit to this lifestyle fully and wholeheartedly. Sometimes, it can be pretty noisy with all of the livestock around, but on some days, it can be deafeningly quiet. It can also be difficult to find instant healthcare if you choose to live far from the central metro. Not everything will be at arm's reach.

When you're living off the land, you will also find that bugs, pests, and other creepy crawlies are a regular thing! It may not be entirely possible to eat outdoors without a screen tent or some form of insect zapper. You have to be able to balance out all of the pros and cons if you're really serious about this lifestyle.

Now, as a modern homesteader, you may still be maintaining a regular job while living off the land. This means not giving up everything in favor of a tiny cabin in the woods. There's certainly an appeal there, as you're essentially enjoying the best of both worlds. But before you dive right into this life, ask yourself the following questions:

- Am I committed enough to go all the way without quitting halfway?

- Am I okay with food that may not be the best tasting ones in order to survive?

- Can I stomach not being able to indulge in modern pleasures every day?

- Am I okay with not having a lot of human interaction on a daily basis?

- Do I have enough funds to push through with this kind of lifestyle, especially during emergencies?

- Do I have enough resources to survive for the first few months as I'm starting out?

- Do I have a backup plan in case things go south, medically, and essentials-wise?

- Do I have basic knowledge of first aid just in case medical help isn't available right away?

- Can I keep a cool head under pressure?

- Do I have the patience to try and solve problems as best as I can?

- Can I handle transitioning gradually into this lifestyle without losing hope that things may seem to be going nowhere?

IV. Building Your Homestead from Scratch

If you've properly weighed the pros and cons of living this self-reliant life, and you're ready to go all-in, congratulations and welcome! You've just embarked on what will probably be the most rewarding journey you will ever experience in your life.

Now, we've already established that sustainable living is easier said and done, and starting out can be incredibly challenging. But armed with the right knowledge and a never-give-up attitude, you can come out of this whole experience unscathed, and even better than ever. Let's dive right in!

A. Step-By-Step Guide to Setting Up

Living off the land is a huge adjustment. To be sure you don't get overwhelmed, let's divide all of your tasks little by little. I'm here to hold your hand as you go through this grand adventure!

1. Getting ready.

Start small.

Yes, it goes without saying that you shouldn't jump right in and tackle the big things first. Start small. Be patient. Go slow. It's not a race—but if it were, then slow and steady wins the race! Pick a project and do it one at a time. The homesteading lifestyle has a long checklist of things you need to accomplish, and it helps to separate everything into bite-sized chunks you can easily digest on a daily basis.

A self-sustaining lifestyle means you should know what you want and how to get it. Don't bite off more than you can chew. It's okay to want to get your feet wet, but don't do several things at once. Plan out a goal for the year, and make it realistic.

Plan your food.

There are so many options when it comes to gardening or livestock, and it's easy to get overwhelmed. First, check the climate where you live. You can start easily with okra, lettuce, Swiss chard, green beans, or summer squash. You can also plant some basil or mint herbs. Bramble fruits like blackberries and raspberries are pretty prolific. Then, as for chickens, they're easier to start with than other animals. All of these are also pretty easy to start with if you're a backyard gardener, and you don't immediately have a huge plot of land to work with, which brings us to my next point.

Know all about the property.

What kind of property do you want to work with? Do you already have a plot of land that you own, or do you plan to buy one? It's just good common sense not to immediately invest in a huge area of land at the very beginning. You can always test things out first. You can make a few raised garden beds first, or practice composting. This will help you get the hang of the basics of gardening before you really get your hands dirty, so to speak. Ask your landlord first before doing any gardening in your rental accommodations!

To get started, you can head to farmer's markets to buy a few seeds for veggies and herbs. Manage the size of your lot with how much you want to plant. You won't be able to raise any cattle in the backyard or in rental accommodations, so study up on your town's regulations regarding livestock and poultry first.

2. Where to find land.

Here's the truth: affordable land is incredibly rare in the United States. If you go and make a quick search online, you will find that there are tons of resources claiming that there are acres and acres of free or cheap land you can acquire for homesteading, but the harsh reality is that nothing can be farther from the truth.

It's difficult to acquire a good chunk of land for a reasonable price but to help you out, there are a few ideas where you can at least start your search. State and local initiatives are generally better options for homesteaders rather than the wild and remote lands from the Bureau of Land Management.

Also, it's important to manage your expectations. No land is completely free—you will still need to spend a good chunk of money in order to develop your plot or install the most important basics like sewage and running water. You may also be required to pledge to reside in that place for specific periods of time, ranging from 5-10 years. Make sure that you're thinking long-term if you do decide to buy the land. Also, don't forget to consult a financial professional to help you manage your acquisition—they know what they're doing!

First off, Kansas is the most popular choice when it comes to affordable land for homesteading. For instance, Lincoln, Kansas, offers reduced property taxes for the first ten years. You can inquire from the local government about homesteading handouts, but always be mindful of any strings attached.

Next, Marquette, Kansas, also has a "free land program," but as I mentioned, nothing is entirely free—you need to pay for sewage installation, water lines, and a bunch of special requirements. Plenty of homesteaders have already established themselves here, so you'd best inquire while you still can.

In Osborne, Kansas, you can also find free property programs for commercial and light industrial purposes, but you can always check to see if homesteading is accepted in a specific area. Over at Rooks County, Kansas, the rules state that you have to have a construction deal within six months after you obtain your plot. You also have to follow procedures on the preconditions of the city. They also have a Neighborhood Revitalization Plan that offers property tax rebates for big savings.

In New Hampshire, you can enjoy a good climate and reliable legal protection. In New Richland, Minnesota, you can benefit from affordable land programs that offer a Tax Increment Financing scheme, where you can spread out your payments over 15 years.

On the other hand, Alaska is known for its wide-open spaces and general untamed beauty. Rural land is sometimes sold for cheap prices here, but you have to be ready for the isolation and the extreme weather when you're homesteading.

There is also a good land program in Marne, Iowa. They've been "giving out" 80 feet x 120 feet lots for a while now, but beware—there's a meticulous list of requirements that you need to be able to fulfill. Also, most plots ban livestock, so if you're looking to raise poultry and cattle, you might be better off looking elsewhere.

Nebraska also has a good number of plausible options for homesteaders. For instance, Curtis, Nebraska features beautiful rolling hills and plots that already come with paved streets, so that's already a big plus for the budding homesteader. In Loup City, Nebraska, you can avail of the "Workforce Home" plan and commit to building your house there along with upfront deposits. It's a good program to consider for low-income individuals.

3. What to consider.

It can be pretty overwhelming to buy land for homesteading, so it's important to know what you're looking for when you inquire. After all, buying land is a huge investment—it's not something you decide to do overnight.

First things first—think about whether or not the land has insurable access. Just because the plot of land has a road leading up to it doesn't mean you can access it willy-nilly. Not everyone will be given the right to access certain roads, especially if the plot of land is surrounded by public plots like the forestry service of the army corps of engineers. The land may also not be subdivided properly, which can be pretty common in large ranches.

If you have an agent working with you, make sure that you check the easement clause in the legal document. You have to be absolutely sure that you can access your own property, and that your right to access it cannot be revoked at any point. You also have to make sure that the access is easy—do you need a 4x4 to get to the land? How near is the maintained public road? Are the roads blocked during certain seasons? How will the weather conditions affect the land's accessibility?

Speaking of getting landlocked, you should also check if there are any covenants and other restrictions on the property. The same is true with water access—make sure you have the right to access the water supply, especially if they're natural sources. Just because there's a creek nearby doesn't always mean you can help yourself to it whenever you please.

If there's no natural water source, make sure you check how deep the wells of the surrounding properties go. You need to plan where your well will be located—this is especially important if you're planning to raise livestock. A good agent should also be able to help you liaise with the local government regarding these issues.

Depending on the county, there will be different minimum septic requirements. Will you only need a composting toilet, or will you be required to have a privately maintained septic system of a specific size? How will you get rid of the waste? Laws will vary depending on the location of your plot.

You should also check if you have any timber and mineral rights. Timber rights are normally given to you, so you have to check whether or not there are any existing timber contracts on your plot. Also, while fixer-uppers look like a good deal, you have to make sure you have enough strength, energy, time, money, and patience to salvage whatever you can.

That said, it's important to check how close the property is to the nearest town, or how easy it is to access utilities. You should also check for alternative power sources just in case you can't reach the utilities in town. This doesn't apply to those who still wish to live in suburban towns without being too isolated from society, but it's still good practice to know how and where you can access your basic necessities.

Here's another huge thing to consider—the neighbors! While you don't want to be too far removed from civilization and other human beings, you also don't want to have nosy neighbors who bug you all the time.

Find out all you can about the community first and decide if there are any issues that you can let slide. Especially with homesteaders, a sense of community and support is important.

As for the land itself, you need to make sure that it's not too polluted so that you can actually grow something! Are the fields too far gone with chemical fertilizers and pesticides? Are you in an area of runoff? Is there a source of pollution from livestock upstream, or are there any potential future hazards you should be aware of?

Do you run the risk of getting caught in a mudslide, or is the area prone to wildfires? Is the place prone to soil erosion and floods? While you certainly can't predict natural calamities, you can try and minimize your risk as much as possible. A quick tip: try to survey the land under varying weather conditions so that you can see up-close what the issues are. If you can check how the land is doing after some heavy rains, you can see where the water stands or how the drainage works.

As for the soil itself, check the composition so that you'll know how well your permaculture will thrive. Get a land survey just to be sure—this will also protect your livestock from wandering into property lines and such.

Finally, ask yourself if you can actually afford the land! Make sure that you will be able to get the land financed. Because some banks may be hesitant to finance vacant land as opposed to one with a structure already built on it, working with an agent is crucial. They will typically have more knowledge about mortgage brokers and whether or not you can get a construction loan, so make sure that your agent is really someone you can trust.

4. Prepping the soil.

Let's say you already bought the land of your dreams, and you're ready to start homesteading! The very first thing you need to take care of is the soil—after all, that's where you'll be doing all your planting.

Now, you may have heard about cultivating the soil and tilling it, but what exactly is the difference between the two? Cultivating is basically breaking up the soil and loosening it for planting. You need to remove the weeds and loosen the soil in order to make room for air, water, and nutrients to penetrate through. It helps you maximize the retention of essential nutrients.

Because of exposure to the elements, the soil can easily dry up and get crusty. Cultivating the soil can not only enhance the absorption of water, but it also lets the microorganisms in the soil do their job at improving the nutrients for the plants. Plus, if you have seedlings, these newly germinated seeds can sprout through the surface more easily with loosened soil.

Just as seedlings benefit from cultivated soil, young weed sprouts also burst through to the surface, making it easier to get rid of them! You wouldn't want the weeds to compete with your plants for nutrients and water, after all.

How exactly do you cultivate the soil? Remember to loosen just a couple of inches deep to make sure that the surface doesn't dry out faster. Be careful not to disturb the roots of the plants and damage them! To steer clear of any root damage, cultivate between rows and only when you observe that the surface of the soil has crusted over. Don't cultivate the soil when it's wet! Only do so when you're planting new seeds, or when you're top dressing the soil with compost.

Now that we've discussed all about cultivating, what about tilling? It's actually a type of deep cultivation that cultivates about 8-10 inches deep. You need to till the soil when you want to prep for a new garden bed. You can also till when you're readying your garden for big amounts of organic material.

Normally, you till about 4-8 inches at the end of the growing season when you're mixing soil amendments. For instance, you can till during the fall so that you can supplement the soil properly with rough organic amendments. These will slowly decompose over the winter and can prep your plants for the next season.

You normally till the soil when it has become compacted because of foot traffic, rain, or other factors over the years.

Loosening the soil for air penetration is especially useful for clay soil. A lot of people also practice no-till gardening so as not to disturb the soil as much as possible, but it may not be too practical for backyard gardeners.

The important thing is to observe how your soil stays healthy! This all requires a lot of trial and error, and some may be blessed with perfect soil while some are not. Your soil may be too sandy, too acidic, or too stony, but as long as you understand the components of healthy soil, you'll eventually get the hang of it.

So what exactly are those components? Soil may just be random organic matter and weathered rock, but the thing that makes healthy soil thrive is actually the life that you can't see—the happy little microorganisms hidden underneath. Yes, these are the worms, insects, small critters, and microbes! When everything is balanced, they help the soil—and your plants—flourish.

As for the soil type, you will have large sand particles, clay, or silt, which are composed of medium-sized particles. The texture of your soil will be determined by the proportion of these particles, which, in turn, affects how your soil drains and how it absorbs nutrients.

Organic matter will help bind these soil particles together. They will normally be made from partially decomposed remains of different plant life, as well as other organisms. The way they bind the particles of the soil will determine how the granules allow air and water to be absorbed and travel throughout the soil. These organisms will also help your soil retain moisture, as well as serve as the food for various forms of life and other microorganisms in the soil.

Because organic matter is essential for keeping your soil healthy, you can increase the organic matter content of your soil by adding aged animal manure, compost, cover crops, peat moss, or mulches. You normally have to add these on the top six inches of the soil, as this upper layer is where most plant roots and soil life are located. Be wary of high-carbon material, though! Soil microorganisms will digest leaves, straw, sawdust, and wood chips by using plenty of nitrogen, and they just might deprive your veggies of it eventually.

Air is also an incredibly important component of healthy soil. You need about 25% of air in your soil to allow the microorganisms to survive. To make sure that your soil is well-aerated, allow pore space between crumbs in the soil. Sand tends to have larger pore spaces compared to clay or slit, but too much air can also be detrimental to your soil, as it can lead to faster decomposition of organic matter. Keep a healthy balance of air by not stepping on the growing beds! Try not to compact the soil with heavy equipment, especially when the soil is wet.

Now, pore space will also dictate the water supply for your plants. The root zone and subsoil will greatly benefit from larger pore spaces, but if there is too much drainage, gravity will draw out the water fast. Now, while smaller pore spaces help water to go through capillary action and migrate back up if the spaces are too waterlogged, the soil organisms get suffocated without any air.

Does it sound like such a meticulous thing to do, maintaining the soil? Don't worry—it may seem overwhelming and frustrating (too much or too little is a crime, and perfect balance is hard to achieve!), but the thing is that most plants are actually more resilient than you think. As long as you do everything to the best of your ability, your beloved veggies will eventually cooperate and thrive, too!

5. Soil types and how to improve them.

How do you identify the type of soil you have in the first place? Gritty soil is sandy, smooth soil is silty, and "slippery when wet" soil is clay. While these are their characteristics in general, it helps to identify your soil type specifically and know how to improve them for the best results.

To check your soil type, simply fill up a quart jar with approximately a third full with some topsoil. Add water into it to fill up the jar to the brim. Close the lid and shake the jar as much as you can! Keep doing so with vigor until you dissolve all the clumps of soil. As you set the jar down, observe how the larger particles sink down to the bottom of the jar. After about a minute or so, the sand portion should have settled at the bottom. Mark this level of soil on the jar. Leave the jar on the windowsill for a few hours. Eventually, silt particles, as they are finer, will settle on top of the sand.

Keep the jar as it is overnight. Clay will eventually sit on top of the silt, so mark the layer's thickness as well. Lastly, the organic matter should sit on top of the clay, or should be floating in the water.

If you have sandy soil, your soil particles will be larger and be made of bits of rock that are shaped irregularly. You will have a bigger air space which will let air and water flow more quickly. This will also make nutrients drain away more easily, so your veggies might get deprived of the nutrients they need. Even when the soil particles are wet, they don't tend to stick together.

To improve this type of soil, you need to work in some organic matter (about three to four inches) in there. Use finished compost or some well-rotted manure and work it into the soil. To help retain the easily draining moisture in the soil, use wood chips, bark, straw, hay, or leaves to mulch around your plants. This will also help cool the soil for you. Every year keep adding about two more inches of organic matter into your soil.

As for clay soil, you will normally have smaller and flatter particles. They are usually packed more tightly together, keeping pore space at a minimum. Clay can be especially difficult to work with when it's wet—the water is drained so slowly that it often gets waterlogged for long periods of time. This also means that the soil is low in microbial activity and organic matter because of the limited air. The roots of the plants will also have a difficult time pushing through the soil because everything is compacted.

Clay will most likely be rich in minerals, so all you have to do is to improve the soil texture to maximize them for your plants. Try to work about two to three inches of the organic matter first, then work about an inch onto the surface every year afterward. If you can, do so in the fall. Also, try to use permanent raised beds so that you can effectively improve the drainage. Till or spade as less as possible.

For silty soil, you will have bits of weathered rocks that are irregularly shaped. This will normally be dense and have small pore spaces, so draining isn't at its best. They do tend to be more fertile than sandy soil or clay. To improve your silty soil, keep adding an inch of organic matter into the soil surface annually. Make sure that you focus on the top few inches to eliminate surface crusting. Also, try not to till often, and avoid walking on the garden beds unnecessarily. It will also help if you construct raised beds.

Now, let's talk about soil pH levels. You can check the relative acidity or alkalinity of your soil with a pH test, which will tell you the ratio of hydrogen (positive) ions to hydroxyl (negative) ions. Neutral pH means that the hydrogen and hydroxyl ions are equally present with a pH of 7. Acidic soil has a pH of 1-6.5, while alkaline soil has a pH of 6.8-14 with more hydroxyl ions.

Plants will grow best in soil that has pH levels of 6.5 to 6.8. When the soil pH is lower or higher than this range, the nutrients in the soil will tend to bind chemically to the particles in the soil, depriving your plants' roots. You want to keep your soil as fertile as possible with this pH range, but it's not a good idea to change your soil pH overnight. This has to be done gradually over a whole growing season or two—once you hit the sweet spot, you just have to maintain it with organic matter.

So, how do you change your soil acidity? If your land is in the eastern half of the U.S., chances are your soil will be more acidic. You can raise the pH of the soil by adding some powdered limestone in the fall to give your soil enough time to adjust to the new alkalinity. Wood ash will also get the job done, but it can raise the pH at a faster rate and cause an imbalance in soil nutrients. Make sure you wait for winter before you apply wood ash. Add about two pounds every 100 square feet approximately every two or three years.

If your land is in the western U.S., your soil will normally be more alkaline. You can add ground sulfur to acidify your soil or add organic materials like peat moss, oak leaves, conifer needles, or sawdust.

B. All About Animals

So far, we've been talking all about improving your soil for gardening, but what about for livestock? Before you add animals to your homestead, make sure that your location is viable for raising them first! You should have secure housing or suitable fencing to keep your livestock safe.

Chickens, for instance, need coops with proper ventilation along with roosts and nest boxes. You can build an open shed for pigs, but you will also need some form of electric fence to keep the pigs from wandering off.

You should also know about any natural predators in your area. You can check with your neighbors or your agent so that you can properly beef up your wire fencing for any specific animal you might want to raise.

Make sure that you have an easy way to give your animals some water supply, even under harsh weather conditions.

During extreme weather and subfreezing temperatures, it can be a challenge to bring water to your livestock—not to mention power outages are common during storms. You should have water reserves ready just in case the worst happens.

1. Different homestead animals.

As for the kind of animal you want to start with, it will really depend on your preferences and on where your homestead is. If you're an urban homesteader, your choices will be extremely limited as the town government will likely set limitations to the animals you can raise.

What's common among all animals is the fact that they will need to be cared for every single day. You have to have the patience and energy to tend to their needs and to clean up after them to keep them healthy and happy.

Below, I'll jot down a quick list on the different animals you can raise and what you need to do to tend to them so that you can make a more informed decision:

Poultry

Chickens and ducks are especially useful for laying eggs. To care for them, you should be able to clean the coop regularly, as well as bring water to the coop manually when needed. You should have the physical strength to hold and carry a chicken for medical care, as well as have the time to freshen the water supply twice a day. You will be removing old feed and replenishing their supply daily as well.

You need to clean the coop every week. Expect to go through about 50 lbs. of layer rations for approximately 12-15 adult hens in an enclosed pen, which will set you back about $12-$16 every week.

Costs of feeds for free-range chickens are lower, but free-range chickens are prime targets for raccoons and foxes. Still, chickens are easier to raise for newbie homesteaders.

Rabbits

Rabbits are similarly easier to raise, and you'll go through about 5 lbs. of feed every week. They tend to eat more during winter, but your feed costs should be between the range of $3-$8 every week if you include fresh rations like apples, bananas, carrots, and leafy greens.

You should be mindful of checking the water supply twice a day, especially during the cold seasons. Be sure to do some regular nail clipping, and be absolutely certain that their hutch is secure if you don't want them to be predator bait!

Goats

Goats are especially useful for milk and meat. It's important to have enough physical strength (or at least a helping hand) for when you need to lift up a goat onto a stand whenever you need to examine it further, shear its fiber, or give it some medication. You need to set aside a full half-hour twice a day to check fences, feed the goats, and give them water. Clean the stall area every week, replace their bedding, and remove any hay that's soiled.

Goats generally tend to cost you about $13-$18 on an average for a full bag weighing 50 lbs. of commercial goat chow. Use approximately half a cup for each goat, two times each day. They also need to have vaccinations each year, so it's a good idea to have a veterinarian on your contact list for the rabies vaccine. About two to four times annually, perform some hoof trimming for your goats as well.

Pigs

Piggies! They're always a favorite among homesteaders, but beware—they're really messy! You need to have relatively more strength when tending to them compared to when you're caring for other animals, as you will be cleaning a lot more. Pigs also tend to get aggressive when it comes to food and can be pushy at times.

You need to spend a lot of time reinforcing fences—electric ones are a must. You can use a lot of different feeds tough, like kitchen scraps, hay, garden waste, and commercial feed. Still, if you're a newbie homesteader, pigs, while popular, may not be the best first choice. It's better to get the hang of raising other animals first before you venture into pig raising.

Cows

Finally, cows! You need to have a whole lot of physical strength for this one. Strong fencing is a necessity, and you need to have enough pasture space for them. You will average about $11-$14 for every bag of grains. They don't generally require too much daily care, but of course, if you're a suburban homesteader without enough space, cows are totally out of the question.

2. More about chickens.

Since it's easier for a newbie homesteader to start off with chickens, I'll get into more detail about them. You can also raise backyard flocks if you don't own a lot of spacious land. You can house chickens with conventional housing systems— you just need mesh cages or solid metal poultry cages with a sloped floor. This can already house about three to eight birds, with water provided using an overhead system. You can set the feed in a trough at the front.

If you want to build backyard chicken coops, you can add perches, windows, and lighting. To keep the chickens cool during the hotter seasons, you can also add green roofs with drought-resistant plants.

Complete feed for chickens already have vitamins, minerals, energy, protein, and other nutrients. This should maximize egg production and overall bird health. It's best to feed your chicks with a high-protein starter diet, starting from right after they hatch up until they reach six to eight weeks old. Afterward, you need to switch up their diet to a more energy-based feed rather than a protein-rich feed.

Poultry diets that contain protein normally consist of beans (like soybeans) and peas. Make sure that they are processed by roasting or steaming, as raw beans may inhibit certain enzymes that contribute to good digestion. Some feeds also include antibiotics, giving chickens a steady dose with scheduled feedings.

Speaking of meds, be wary of the chicken disease called Coccidiosis—a mild case in mature chickens can lead to resistance. Normally, you can use a coccidiostat feed with chickens until they're 16 weeks old before switching to normal feeds.

As for chicken breeds, the Ameraucana, Buff Cochin, and the Silver Laced Wyandotte lay eggs wonderfully. They're docile and can also make for good pets! The White Leghorn, in particular, produces large white eggs, while the Black Copper Maran can produce chocolate brown eggs.

C. The Costs of Homesteading

Here's the reality of the situation: while homesteading and sustainable living sound exciting and fun, there are real costs involved—and they're not easy to shell out. You can save money on some of your projects if you get creative, but there are still costs you just won't be able to escape.

You can always procure a few tools second-hand from online forums and other channels like Craigslist or at thrift stores. Pre-loved goods help you live a more sustainable life, too, after all! Still, expect the costs of repairs or any improvements to be 50% more than what you initially think they will be.

It's a good idea to have another secondary source of income just in case you go through a rough patch, an emergency, or simply a bad year for your crops. Find a space for yourself as well to help you relax and have fun. Don't let the stress get you down! Always find a way to pat yourself on the back after a day's hard work. What's the use of living self-reliance if you don't get satisfaction at the end of the day?

To keep yourself from getting bill shock, make sure you plan your projects one at a time so that your costs are spread out. If you're comfortable having a healthy amount of debt, you can look into your local Home Depot consumer credit card— they often have promotions to help you get started, at the very least. They also have some interest-free options depending on your spending tier—just make sure you pay off your debt before you move on to the next interest-incurring tier.

Every homestead will be different. While I can't give you an exact range for the costs as there is a wide variety of factors that can affect your expenses, I can at least give you a picture of how your monthly expenses will look like. Every month, your budget will likely be composed of the following:

- Rent or Mortgage
- Insurance
- Taxes
- Car Payment
- Gas
- Internet Bills
- Utilities
- Sewer Costs
- Trash Costs
- Personal Necessities
- Food

Rural internet access may be hard to come by, so make sure you check that out when you're choosing your property. Private wells and provisions for solar energy can lower your utility bills, but you'll still probably shell out around $100+ every month. For your land, you will likely shell out approximately $600+ each year, which includes structures, equipment, power tools, and, sadly, taxes. Upkeep can even set you back up to $500 each year.

Food can set you back approximately $100 a month, at the very least, depending on how you consume. You can't grow everything, so you'll still need to buy a few basics like flour, sugar, and salt. You can always buy things in bulk, but they do still cost money.

There's no escaping sickness, either. Medical bills and trips to the vet can cost you around $200+ a year, while initial investments on the animals themselves can cost around $1,000+ starting out. Feeds can go from $15 to $500+ every month.

This may all seem overwhelming, but don't let the costs get you down! You really do have to spend some to make some, and the benefits of homesteading and sustainable living will always outweigh the cons in the long run.

V. Growing Your Own Plants

Growing your own food is incredibly satisfying, and self-reliance inevitably starts with this personal crop culture.

It's easier to set up a garden than an actual animal farm, and you can quickly grow your own veggies from the comfort of your own kitchen or backyard. Even if you live in the city, you can still get busy planting!

A. What is Permaculture?

So, what is permaculture? It's basically a system in which we get self-reliance by growing food anywhere we can, from patio pots to backyard fences. Permaculture lets you create a cycle of turning food waste and dead plants into mulch and compost to help new plant growth. You can mix and match with annuals and perennials depending on your observation of your own plot, backyard, or garden.

You simply need to decide where you want to locate your garden. If you're an urban homesteader, you may or may not have a backyard. If you already have a plot of land in the suburbs, that's great—but if you live in the city, you can also start with your balcony!

Permaculture also means that nothing goes to waste. Your leftover plant matter and kitchen scraps can be turned into compost to make sure that your soil is rich in nutrients for the next season. You can even do some worm composting by placing all of your plant debris into bins with composting worms or even regular earthworms.

The scraps will be consumed by the worms, which will result in worm castings that increase the nutrients in the soil. If you can't capture the worms from your own garden, you can buy them from bait shops near you.

Using a big 5-gallon bucket, make a few holes at the bottom, about the size of a coin each. Bury it in your garden about halfway through. Add some shredded paper or cardboard, and a layer of dried grass or soil.

Common in permaculture, no-dig gardening protects the soil microbiome. Avoiding digging preserves beneficial bacteria and other organisms that keep the soil rich in nutrients.

You can also create a keyhole garden, which is a raised bed that has indentations on one side to help gardeners maintain, water, and weed easily.

There's also such a thing as companion gardening, which promotes biodiversity in gardens. Plenty of crops can complement each other and help each other grow, like beans, squash, and corn. There are just so many ways you can go about your gardening, and they're all incredibly fun!

B. How to Make a Four-Season Garden

The best way to maximize your crops is to plant all year round. Not all crops will survive all kinds of seasons, and if you're truly living a sustainable and self-reliant life, you wouldn't want to waste any season without growing anything.

Climate change is a very real thing. The weather is becoming more and more unpredictable, with harsh seasons getting even harsher. Winters are getting wetter and warmer, and crops bear the brunt of these unsuitable growing climates. During the winter, you can provide a good mulch blanket for your plants to protect the soil from any heavy rain or heavy winds. This will also help insulate the ground whenever there are fluctuations in temperature.

You can install some PVC or plastic sheeting and make it into a small hoop house so that you can protect your plants from inclement weather. If you have the luxury to build a greenhouse, these are also great ways to protect your plants in inhospitable environments.

Now, creating a garden that generates fresh produce for 12 months can be tricky, but with the right seeds for your location, it's possible. You can consult your local Department of Agriculture to check which ones will thrive in your area. Territorial Seed Company, Mary's Heirloom Seeds, and Rareseeds.com are also good resources for seed information. Then, start indoors.

When was the average last frost in your location? From there, count backward. Between 12-14 weeks, you can plant onions, leeks, and chives. With lettuce, peppers, and other cabbage family crops, check for a range from 8-12 weeks. Go for 6-8 weeks for tomatoes and eggplants, and 2-4 weeks for squash, okra, cucumbers, melons, and pumpkins.

Outdoors, you can already start warming up the soil in preparation. A few weeks before you transplant the seedlings you just planted indoors, lay out some sheets of black plastic over your beds. The warmth of the soil should help soil organisms thrive for better root development later on. Be careful not to overheat the soil when it's time to plant your seedlings—make sure you remove the plastic or cover it with mulch when the weather is hot.

You can maximize your harvest with succession planting—this means that as soon as you harvest a certain crop, you quickly fill the space with another new crop. Plant at intervals of one to two weeks using summer crops as a replacement, then fall and winter crops. You can determine your planting date by counting backward from the first frost date. Check the number of days that have elapsed until crops mature, then add 15 days. This is because, in cold weather, plants take a longer time to mature. The number you get is your planting date.

You can start planting indoors for most vegetables except for root crops. These can keep seedlings cool during hot weather—or, you can also plant them under the shade of bigger, more mature crops outside. If you time your plantings right, you can be harvesting even during the supposed downtime of winter.

You should still be very careful when you're harvesting, though! Peas, corn, and beans can be harvested once you observe that the pods or the husks are already completely dry. Make sure that before you shell them, keep them out of direct sunlight and store them first in a warm and dry place for a few weeks.

As for fleshy fruit veggies like tomatoes, squash, cucumbers, and peppers, you can harvest their seed before they start to rot. Pick the seeds by hand, dry them out on a tray, and store them in a glass jar in the fridge.

Planning your continuous harvest is literally planning it out on your calendar so that you're ready for the next season. In late winter, you can clean your cold frames or grow micro-greens there. If you have any winter beds that are not being used, mulch or plant cover crops to improve the soil for next year.

C. How to Harvest Your Veggies (and Eggs If You Have Them)

We talked about how you can make your soil as healthy as can be, and how to maximize the calendar year for succession planting. Now comes the fun part—harvesting! You may think that it's as simple as harvesting whenever something looks ripe and tasty (and often, that's just the way it works!), but there are some tips and tricks to harvesting to make sure you get the best out of your own produce. Let's talk about the most common veggies.

You should make it a habit of taking your basket out to your garden and checking which ones are ready to harvest every single day. When you harvest veggies as soon as they ripen, you effectively encourage your crops to produce even more veggies. With vegetables, though, it doesn't mean something is better just because it's bigger. Some veggies, like zucchini, tend to toughen up and get woody if they grow more than six or seven inches.

The key thing to remember is that you should have a system of jotting down when you planted what. Seed packets often provide very useful information about what to expect when harvesting. You should also be wary of any red flags like rotting parts or yellowing leaves—remove them as soon as they're discovered.

For plenty of veggies, their varieties will determine when they're ready to harvest, so it's good to have a decent amount of seed knowledge (or a handy seed catalog!) in your back pocket.

To harvest herbs, cut them back frequently or pinch to increase their production of stems and leaves. This will also prevent them from blooming because once they do so, the flavor changes. This is especially true with basil—you need to pinch back frequently to make sure the herb stays productive. If you ever find yourself with a surplus of herbs, you can dry herbs like thyme or oregano in a brown paper bag, or make pesto with basil!

For peppers, once they're full-sized, you can already harvest them while they are still green in color. If you leave them on the vine for too long, they change to red, yellow, orange, or whatever their variety is. Changing colors means that its texture becomes less crisp and will deepen in its flavor—like if a hot pepper changes in color, it will get even hotter. Make sure you know what you're using the peppers for so that you know whether or not to harvest them while they're green.

Lettuce must be harvested before it develops a flower stalk. Once it bolts, the leaves become more bitter. Cut the largest leaves with scissors and wait for the smallest leaves to grow. Protect the lettuce from hot weather with a shade tent or a row cover that's translucent to delay bolting.

For green beans, harvest them before they reach their maximum size. If the seeds mature, they harden, and the pod toughens, which isn't the best way to enjoy them. Also, wait until the green beans are dry before picking them, so steer clear of the morning dew on the vines. In the same way, garden peas that are left too long will become stringy and tough. Pick out a pod and test to see if it's already round but tender.

For watermelons, check to see if the bottom of the melon turns yellowish. This means that it will be close to being ripe enough, with a tougher rind. Eventually, you will also have to test one out and cut it open, using it as a basis for the rest of the bunch. Make sure that you cut the melons from their vines and not just pull them off. The same is true with cucumbers, as they get dry and woody if they're left on the vine for too long. Everything has to be timed just right!

As for root vegetables, the seed packet will be very crucial. Very gently, you can loosen the soil and check if your beets, radishes, carrots, parsnips, and turnips are ready to be pulled up depending on their size. If root crops are smaller, the flavor is more delicate; older ones have a tougher and woodier taste.

Now, I know we're talking about crops here, but I'd just like to talk a little bit about harvesting eggs too, especially if you're a newbie homesteader starting off with chickens. You always have to make sure that the eggs are clean and fresh, whether they're for your own personal consumption or you're planning to sell them somewhere.

When you gather eggs, try to do so often and early, like twice every day, to make sure they're clean. You should also gather eggs often to keep the chickens from eating the eggs! If you leave the eggs there for too long, they might get broken, the hens may step on them, or they might become stained with poop.

Make sure that your nest boxes are feathered well and with plenty of straw lining and shavings. If you keep nest boxes clean and remove any soiled eggs or broken eggs right away, you encourage the hens to lay their eggs there even more.

To clean the eggs you've harvested, you can do either dry cleaning or wet cleaning. With dry cleaning, you keep the bloom (the natural antibacterial layer of the eggs) intact. This will also let you keep the eggs even if they're unrefrigerated. All you have to do is to use a loofah, any abrasive sponge, or fine sandpaper to clean the eggs and remove any feces or dirt.

In case there's any yolk that's stuck to the outside of the egg, you need to do wet cleaning for the shells. Use warm running water to clean the shells and use a paper towel to dry them. You can also spray the eggs with a sanitizing solution of bleach and water, then place them in a wire rack or an open carton.

After cleaning and drying the eggs, pack them in egg cartons and label them with the date they were collected. It's best to refrigerate the eggs to make them last longer, up to about a month after the collection date. Wash dry, cleaned eggs immediately before you cook them.

To test if eggs are still fresh, fill up a bowl with water and check if the egg floats. If it does, it's likely already spoiled—you can compost it to make sure nothing is wasted.

VI. Indoor Permaculture

I know I've already briefly touched upon growing indoor plants, but it's just so incredibly fun and easy to do that I think the whole idea merits a section of its own! You can grow your own herbs from the comfort of your own home even if you're in a suburban homestead, or you're a city dweller looking to live a more sustainable life.

Herbs need plenty of sunlight, which can be an issue if you're growing them indoors. You will also need a potting medium that drains well, so it can be messy if you don't know where to place them.

A. Setting Up, Location, and Watering

The most common location indoors would be anywhere near a window that gets a minimum of three hours of sun every day, preferably midday or afternoon sunlight.

Make sure that you don't bring the plant too close to the glass to keep it from getting burnt up and receiving poor airflow. Try to have a space of about a foot from the glass window to protect it from harsh and direct sunlight.

In a pot with enough draining holes, fill with potting mix and not soil. You can place a saucer under the pot to keep from making a mess as long as you make sure that you can still let the excess water drain properly to avoid flooding the plant. Waterlogged roots will rot, so a tray of water definitely won't do you any good.

Most herbs don't need a great deal of water, either, so watering about once every week should suffice. You won't need fertilizer for about three months or so with a high-grade premium potting mix. When spring starts, try to feed with slow release powders, pellets, or granule fertilizer at least once every year, and adjust the frequency if you're often harvesting them. It also helps to re-pot them every two years to keep the potting mix fresh.

When you're looking for the perfect spot to place your plant, it doesn't do to simply look for any window sill—the sunlight has to have the right frequencies to grow your plants well. Preferably, pick a south-facing or west-facing window so that the plants can maximize the light that the sun gives off as it passes over. Apps like Sun Surveyor and SunCalc can help you track the hours of sunlight every window gets in your house.

You can also install a grow light—whether they're fluorescent or LED arrays, they can help provide enough energy to help leafy greens like parsley, basil, ad lettuce thrive. LED lights will initially cost you more, but they will have bigger energy savings in the long run and will produce healthier plants eventually.

If you have the funds for it, you can also install retrofit solar tubes to make sure that sunlight streams through your interiors from the roof. Fiber optic cables can transport the light well into your house up to as much as 50 feet inside.

Planting indoors also poses the challenge of keeping your plants well-hydrated. Most modern homes have air pumped through vents to keep interiors cool, but this also increases water evaporation for the plants, drying them out.

You need to water them constantly, or you can mulch with coffee grounds to delay evaporation rates somehow. You can also buy or make your own self-watering planter for hassle-free results!

Self-watering planters have a water reservoir underneath the pot and separate from the soil. You can also use a pump with an automated timer, and as you set the time, the pump automatically squirts water into the pot as needed.

As for the soil, you can use non-soil blends that have coconut coir, perlite, biochar vermiculite, or peat moss. While you want to make sure that you have a healthy ecology in your soil, growing plants indoors also means that an overabundance of fungi and spores can lead to breathing issues and allergies inside the house.

It's best to have larger pots and to use the basic earthworm, about one or two for each large pot to regulate moisture and proper bacterial growth.

B. What to Grow

Indoor gardens are usually composed of salad greens and herbs you can readily use in the kitchen.

They're easy to grow and easy to harvest, and you can simply pluck the amount you need and encourage the plant to grow more leaves as you do.

1. Basic herbs

Aside from rosemary, sage, thyme, oregano, and mint, you can also grow basil, especially during the summer. In case of any surplus, you can always make pesto and stock them up in the fridge for those pasta cravings on weeknights.

Cuban oregano or Spanish thyme can be pretty easy to maintain as well—it can even survive through minor neglect.

2. Chili peppers and ginger

If you're the type who just loves all things hot and spicy, peppers not only look really good as decorative plants, but they also taste amazing as they happily grow inside your home. Ginger, on the other hand, is easy to grow as it prefers the shade. It's highly medicinal too, and it likes humidity.

3. Dwarf citrus trees

Small citrus plants grow well inside—and you can't really resist a healthy slice of zesty lemon, right?

The cool thing about citrus trees is that they have parthenocarpy, which is the ability to produce fruit even if they're not pollinated. This makes them a good candidate for indoor gardening with the most productivity.

4. Pitaya or dragon fruit

Planted from seed, the pitaya not only produces delicious fruit, but it also has pretty flowers that emit a nice fragrance throughout the house. You can also just grow regular cactus and other succulents—they're the perfect indoor plants that can withstand neglect.

5. Lemongrass

Lemongrass is that easy to grow in the sense that you don't even plant it in soil! You can simply buy a stalk from the market, making sure that the base is still intact.

Then, just trim the top and dunk it in a few inches of water. The stalk will soon produce roots on its own and a few more shoots for you.

6. Chives

Chives are pretty prolific, and they don't need much sunlight to grow. Simply planting a bunch with roots into potting soil will keep it growing.

Don't forget to cut one-third or so off the top to help stimulate new growth every so often.

7. Mint

Be wary of spearmint and peppermint as they can easily choke out other herbs with how invasive they can be! They're that easy to grow, and you need to harvest them often. It's better to plant with seeds instead of scraps. Peppermint will also do well in the shade—just make sure you give it some sunlight every day for just a little bit.

8. Chamomile

Best for use in tea, chamomile can also be an ingredient in herbal medicine and can calm the nerves effectively. It can also help with inflammation and stomach aches—plus, you can even "cure" the plant next to it with its fertilizing properties. Known as "the plant's physician," chamomile has roots that can dredge up potassium, phosphorus, and calcium, keeping your soil healthy as can be.

9. Lavender

Lavender is easy to grow as they don't need that much tending to. You can use them as a condiment in salads or use them to soothe insect bites and other aromatherapy needs. They smell really good too! They grow best in well-drained soil that's warm, and under full sunlight.

10. Aloe vera

Known for its healing properties for skin problems and for soothing burns, aloe vera is very handy in the kitchen. It can also help with good digestion and must be in full sun or under light shade. You can easily keep it near a sunny window indoors—just make sure you protect it from frost as they're very sensitive to that!

11. Dandelion

Now, you might think that dandelions are simply weeds that you want nowhere near your garden, but they actually have good uses as fertilizer. With their long taproots, they can reach deep into the subsoil and store nutrients in their leaves, making them excellent fertilizers when the leaves die and decompose. As they accumulate calcium, phosphorus, and potassium, you can cut back the leaves and let them contribute to healthy plant growth.

Dandelions also encourage the earthworms to thrive. You can have them outdoors in your garden as well under fruit trees if you have them. Try to snip off the leaves once every month to keep the dandelions from flowering. You wouldn't want them to seed and end up taking over your garden.

Also, the dandelion greens are actually edible—add them to your salad mix and partake of their accumulated nutrients as well!

If your dandelions do end up going to seed, you can add the seeds to your foraging seed mix to keep your chickens happy and healthy. If the dandelions end up flowering, they can attract pollinators to your garden. If you dry the roots, they can also be used as a medicinal tonic for your liver and kidneys.

VII. Preservation and Storage

After growing and harvesting all the fruits of your hard work, you should also know how to preserve and store them properly. After all, you're not going to be able to consume everything right after harvest. There are many ways to preserve food, and if you really want to be self-reliant, you need to make sure you can keep the meat and veggies that you grow for a long, long time.

Among the most common ways you can preserve your food is to can them. You can also dehydrate them, ferment, infuse, or dry cure—the possibilities are endless! Preserving your harvest makes sure that nothing goes to waste, and that you can remain properly stocked even during emergencies and rough patches.

A. Freezing

Freezing is the most popular form of food preservation, and for a good reason—it's easy to freeze food no matter where you are. You can use a freezer to preserve anything from meats to veggies—even dairy. You need to use electricity, though, and when the power goes out, you'll definitely be in a pinch.

Before freezing anything, make sure you wash them and remove any dirt or debris. Blueberries, for instance, can freeze really well—just throw them into freezer bags, and they're good to go. For peaches and mangoes, you need to flash freeze them first before you pack them into freezer bags. Do the same for banana slices, or you can even put them in the freezer whole and just thaw them later on.

Broccoli, green beans, carrots, snap peas, shelled peas, and cauliflower need to be blanched first. Pumpkin, winter squash, tomatoes, diced cooked potatoes, and chopped up herbs freeze really well without much fuss. You can also freeze poultry, seafood, meat, milk, cheese, cream, and butter.

B. Cold cellars

There are also food items that don't freeze well, such as cucumbers, uncooked potatoes, and raw veggies. You can do some root cellaring or cold cellaring if you do have a cellar or cold room in your location. You don't need any prep work for this, so pumpkins, cabbages, potatoes, garlic, onions, and apples can be preserved as they are.

For garlic and onions, you can hang them to dry and store in an open basket for air circulation. You can't, however, store raw meat, raw dairy, berries, tomatoes, peppers, and fleshy fruit in cold cellars long-term.

C. Water bath canning

If you don't have any special equipment, water bath canning should be easy for you. You simply need a canning rack and a large stockpot. You need to have Mason jars, of course, and it helps if you have canning tool kits as well. This is a great way to preserve pickles, salsa, jellies, canned fruit, sauces, and pie filling. You can basically can most acidic fruits and vegetables, as long as they have a PH level of 4.6 or less.

So how do you get started with water bath canning? In the bottom of a tall pot (perhaps a lobster pot or any stockpot), place a rack in order to help keep the bottom of your jars elevated from the pan's own bottom. This will let the evaporating water escape and can keep your jars safe from breaking.

Cover the jars with water up to approximately an inch above the lid. Heat up the water up to 140 F for raw-packing or 180 F for hot-packing. Make sure that all of your jars are in good condition without any chips and other imperfections. Clean the jars thoroughly before filling them up, but don't fill them to the brim—leave about 1/4" or 1" of headspace.

When you lower the jars into the water bath, be very careful not to burn yourself! Use tongs or a jar lifter and lower the jars vertically. Your recipe for canning particular food items will tell you how long you should time the process. Afterward, let the jar cool slowly—don't place the jars immediately onto a counter to prevent temperature shock. Do not disturb the jars for about 12 to 14 hours.

Water bath canning is great for raspberries, currants, mulberries, strawberries, blueberries, blackberries, mangoes, cherries, plums, peaches, pears, grapes, pineapple, apples, and pickled veggies. These must be pickled before water bath canning and can include green beans, cauliflower, cucumbers, asparagus, and carrots.

Meat, fish, and poultry are not safe for water bath canning! You shouldn't can eggs and dairy either.

D. Pressure canning

There are plenty of tested pressure canning recipes you can search for online to make sure you do everything safely. You wouldn't want to run the risk of blowing up your own kitchen!

This official guide from Ball and Kerr can actually give you a safe and detailed guide on canning 101 better than I can. But let me tell you that as mentioned, meat and poultry must be pressure canned.

E. Dehydrating

If you're a complete newbie and you don't want to screw things up, dehydrating is totally foolproof! It's less intimidating and has a lower chance of causing your family food poisoning from improperly handled procedures.

You can either dry food under the sun as in sundried tomatoes and raisins or use your oven at home. You can also invest in an at-home food dehydrator for fuss-free dehydrating. Here, you can simply set the time and lay your food out for the dehydrator to do its thing without the need for you to keep an eye on it. You can go with anything from kale chips to apple slices and keep the healthy snacks coming!

You can also dehydrate meat and fish for jerky, as well as leafy greens like spinach so you can make powder and add them to stews and sauces. If you want to dehydrate potatoes, make sure that you slice them and blanch them first before you dehydrate them.

On the other hand, you shouldn't dehydrate eggs, milk, butter, avocadoes, and fatty meat.

F. Infusing

By immersing certain herbs in a given solvent, you are essentially creating an infusion—while this really isn't a way of preserving the actual food per se, it can preserve the flavor and the nutrients of that particular food into the liquid solvent. Here, you discard the solid components and instead keep the liquid infusion or extract. The extract can be used in medicine and even in personal care products.

Your liquid solvent can be water, honey, vinegar, glycerin, or alcohol. It's important that you follow safety precautions when you're infusing herbal oils. You can also infuse fruit in alcohol and vinegar or garlic and onions in vinegar. Citrus fruit rinds, hot peppers, and roots like turmeric and ginger can also be infused in alcohol or vinegar.

G. Dry curing

To successfully inhibit the growth of bacteria, people have been using salt and sugar for years and years. You can cure meats like salami, jerky, ham, and bacon via salting, as well as preserve herbs and citrus fruits.

VIII. How to Sell Your Produce

With everything that you've grown and harvested from your homestead or backyard permaculture garden, you may want to keep everything to yourself—or you may want to make a little money with it!

Fresh produce born from your self-sufficiency and sustainable living is always a great way to start something financially lucrative. Besides—you wouldn't want all that produce to go to waste!

A. Where to Sell Your Surplus

Selling your surplus is a great way for you to make money if you're looking for an alternative source of income. Homesteading might mean you are leaving your regular nine-to-five, or it may lead you to take time apart from your daily work to tend to your homestead. This is why making money off of it is just good common sense—after all, you're already spending time and effort on it, so why not make a little extra cash while you're at it?

Today, there are plenty of ways for you to maximize your surplus. You can not only visit your local farmer's market (you can even sell your own handmade soaps), but you can also consult with your local town hall or chamber of commerce to see what your options are in your area.

There is also such a thing as CSAs (Community Supported Agriculture). Here, you can take advantage of a small scale closed market where buyers enter into relationships with sellers. There is a subscription service from sellers to buyers, allowing the buyer to commit to the products on a certain homestead or farm on a weekly or monthly basis.

You can also be on the lookout for food co-ops, where an organization takes responsibility for bringing locally grown produce to the front door of the buyer. These organizations are normally formed by state or by region, and there are newsletters as well as an official website that details all of the information for each producer or seller. This effectively widens the reach of local homesteaders and provides more efficient coverage for each location.

Of course, these organizations will have a list of requirements you have to fulfill as a seller in order to be included in the group. Rules and regulations may include packaging that is state-inspected or items that are made from a USDA-inspected facility. You may be required to acquire an egg license or other labeling standards, depending on your area.

Once you know where to sell your surplus, it's important to know where you should market them—and the internet is one of the most efficient ways you can do so. It's easy to do and has a wide coverage you otherwise won't be able to reach if you went with manual marketing. You can put up a few items for auction over at eBay, or simply use social media to promote your produce. Fresh and organic producers can check Localharvest.org and Newfarm.org for opportunities, where you can even get free advertising. They offer support in the form of an online store as well, where producers can list items for sale from specialty herbs to homestead crafts.

If your fresh items don't do well with being sold or shipped online, or you simply don't want to sell them via the e-commerce route, you can always set up your own farm stand. You can also complement your online store with your physical store anyway, so it's still a win-win situation.

You can sell your produce right from your own homestead. You can also sell from a truck that's loaded with produce, as long as you get permission from the local government for your portable stand.

B. Legal Aspects of Selling

Wherever you may want to sell your produce, remember that you should have provisions for liability and insurance. Food poisoning and accidents on site may sometimes happen, so it's best to check how your insurance can cover you just in case.

There will be federal and state Cottage Food laws that you need to abide by, whether you're just selling your surplus so that nothing goes to waste or you're making a living out of them. The same is true with the Farm to Consumer Legal Defense Fund—these rules include the requirements for labeling and preparation needed for every state.

The more types of food that you sell, the more laws you need to follow. Selling meat, for instance, can be a bit more meticulous, as USDA-inspected facilities are involved. If you have a small farm and you already know ahead of time which customers want to buy meat from you, then a USDA-inspected and approved facility can butcher the steers. However, there will be no inspector on-site here. The meat will be sold to the customers after the animal has already been butchered, and the weight is determined.

When customers pay you, this means that the ownership of the meat transfers to them. They are the ones who bear the responsibility of picking up the meat from the butchery. They will also pay the butcher's fee, and it will be marked as "NOT FOR SALE" in a method called "customer slaughter." This is the best method to use if you only have a small farm and you know your customers who regularly buy from you every year. If you are selling meat to the general public, you will be required to involve a fully inspected plant.

As for poultry, the chicken can normally be butchered on the farm even without an inspector. Some states also don't require a license and may have a maximum number of birds to be processed and sold directly to the customer. The bottom line is that you need to consult your local area to know the specific rules and regulations when it comes to selling your wares.

It goes without saying that you should always abide by the unspoken rules of fair profit. While you definitely won't be able to compete with the big business chains and the corporate moguls when it comes to competitive prices, you should still keep reasonable prices. If you have quality produce, customers who are well-informed will still turn to you. The nutrition, flavor, and care that go into your products will keep the big systems from bankrupting small farmers and homesteaders.

You can also point out the more humane treatment of the animals in your homestead to help draw more customers to your homestead. Overall, there's a certain personal touch that gives you an edge over the business chains out there, even if your products have a little bit of a more premium price compared to the supermarket-bought alternatives.

It's important to maintain this certain level of quality both in your internal and external processes. As long as you stick to what you love to do (and follow the laws, of course), your tiny homestead can and will stand a chance out there.

IX. Other Ways to Live Sustainably

Sustainable living requires time, patience, and a whole lot of effort—but the rewards are extremely satisfying. Aside from being self-reliant and growing your own food, there are many other ways you can live sustainably today and in all the years to come.

According to the World Health Organization, many annual deaths (approximately 13 million) are caused by environmental factors. A quarter of all kinds of diseases around the world are also due to natural causes in the environment, and these could actually have been avoided or prevented if only we learned to take care of our surroundings.

If you do your own part in taking care of Mother Nature, you are also effectively taking care of the lives of all of the people around you and not just yourself. Better environmental conditions can, for instance, help alleviate sicknesses like asthma, stroke, chronic obstructive pulmonary disease (COPD), cardiovascular disease, and other health issues.

It's really all about living smart—live the way you would if you accepted that we are living with borrowed and finite resources and that these luxuries won't last forever. We all have to do what we can to make sure that we sustain our healthy living in all the generations to come.

Sustainable living doesn't just mean growing your own food, it also helps to make sustainable food choices every single day. The production and processing of packaging, as well as the transportation of food, all contribute highly to the use of chemical fertilizers and the dependency on fossil fuels. This not only affects our health negatively, but they also prove to be highly detrimental to the health of the environment.

Aside from your own produce, you should try to source food or other items that practice responsible choices that minimize the effects on the environment. Consider the impacts of your own choices as a consumer, and choose healthy and environmentally conscious products. For the food items that you don't produce yourself, look for farmers who limit the use of pesticides and those who treat their livestock with humane actions. If you can, pick suppliers who have closer proximity to you so that you can reduce the distance that the items travel from origin to destination. You can also choose to support rural communities as well as pick food items that are free of toxins and are locally grown.

As for your everyday transportation, you can also choose more sustainable means to travel. Vehicles release harmful pollutants and can increase the air pollution levels to unimaginable heights. Air pollution can increase cardiac symptoms and aggravate symptoms of asthma. They affect premature mortality and decrease lung function as well.

You can shift to alternative commute options like walking (the exercise is good for your health!) and riding your bike. If you must, use public transportation and enlist in a carpool service. You can also try remote work arrangements and an alternate work schedule to reduce the frequency of travel.

Inside your own home, you can make greener updates in your own way. For example, if you keep your home well-insulated, you can conserve energy for great cost savings and spend less on air conditioning as well as heat regulation. This will not only help you save the planet, but it will also help you save on your monthly bills.

You can also use a programmable thermostat so that you can set a schedule on your air conditioner or your heat regulator. Prevent air leaks by sealing outside openings, and conserve water by using low-flow faucets or aerating faucets and showerheads. You can also save up to 30% of your energy at home with tankless and on-demand water heaters as opposed to standard natural gas tank heaters.

X. Frequently Asked Questions

Congratulations on reaching the end of this book! By now, you should be a totally savvy and self-sufficient homesteader newbie with a passion for sustainable living. Just to recap, below are some of the most common questions and answers about homesteading so that you can take living off the grid as straightforward as possible.

What is urban homesteading?

This is a type of urban lifestyle that values organic food, recycling, and other homemade delights. This DIY way of living involves growing your own food, whether you're in the suburbs or in the city.

Who can practice urban homesteading?

Anyone can be an urban homesteader! It doesn't matter what you're regularly doing for your career, or what your current lifestyle is. All you need to be sure about are the particular laws that your local town imposes regarding homesteading. Some towns allow raising chickens, while some have restrictions on poultry and livestock. If you live in an apartment, you can grow your own herbs and veggies inside your kitchen as long as you have a sunny windowsill. You may also have container gardens or mini-orchards in your backyard if you have one.

What activities can I pursue when homesteading?

Being a homesteader means you will likely be doing a lot of do-it-yourself projects, which makes each endeavor more worthwhile as you go about it. The end goal of homesteading is to live a more self-sufficient and sustainable life and to become more frugal and independent with your lifestyle.

You will probably be trying your hand at raising chickens, depending on the specific rules of your city or town. Keep your zoning codes in mind, and don't break the law! When you're sure that everything is nice and legal, you will find that raising chickens is immensely satisfying—not to mention you can get free eggs and even a few pets while you're at it!

You will also be doing a lot of gardening and growing your own produce. Just think—who wouldn't want to have fresh fruits and veggies all year round? Plus, growing your own produce means that you're sure about where your greens are coming from. You know they're organic and pesticide-free because you technically raised them from seed to fruit!

Some homesteaders also like to keep bees, but if the idea of breeding them intimidates you, you can simply plant plants that are bee-friendly to make your garden ecosystem thrive. Other people also dip their toes into home brewing so that they and their families can enjoy homemade beer, wine, and spirits from the comfort of their own home.

Other people also make their own soap, cleaning products, and other household essentials! You can even go so far as to make essential oils, candles, and other aromatherapy products for selling and make a little extra cash while you're having fun.

How can I get started with homesteading?

The first thing you need to do is to survey your land or to look for land. If you already have an existing plot, check to

see if your planned homestead activities will be possible—
make sure that your plan is realistic and measurable. Don't
jump into things too quickly, or you might end up
overwhelming yourself.

Research is extremely important, as well as consulting your
local government office. Research online about the available
lands you can look into or ask homesteaders you may know.
Gather enough intel before making a life-altering decision,
and consult your family, of course. You wouldn't want to
uproot their whole life without getting their consent first—
that's just a recipe for disaster from the get-go. Starting a
homestead is a big deal, and it requires commitment not just
from you but from everyone around you. Besides, it will be
easier for you to get started with your homestead when
everyone's on-board—you will definitely need all the help
and support you can get!

What should I look for in a homestead?

Your top priorities should be housing, food, and water. Make
sure you can secure water and food sources once you have
your plot of land to live in. If you're using water off-grid, you
need to make sure that your water is clean and safe to

drink—no use getting poisoned just to live the self-reliant life. You should also have back-up water sources just in case things go south, or whenever there's a drought.

What tools should I have when I'm starting a homestead?

You don't really need any fancy equipment when you're first starting out. You can always start with what you have, even if all you have are containers for seeds and indoor herbs. First, you have to decide what you want to prioritize. Then, you find the tools that you need to accomplish that particular goal.

If you want to prep your soil first, you can use a regular shovel, a garden rake, a hatchet, some basic tools for carpentry, buckets, and a wheelbarrow. You also need watering cans and anything you can think of to repurpose in your home. You need to make do with what you have at first before you can move on to the fancier equipment, but if you have the funds for it, then, by all means, invest in more time-saving tools to make your life easier.

How can I save up to start a

homestead?

There are a lot of costs involved in setting up a homestead, but if you want to go slow and steady, first learn how to give up the things that you don't really need in your everyday life. I mean, do you really need another cup of fancy coffee to go? Or that shiny pair of shoes on sale in the window?

Now, you may think that there are just too many things you need to consider when you're trying to set up a homestead or build your own permaculture from your backyard. While it's true that you will face lots of challenges in this journey, it's also true that there is no cause more worthwhile than this.

The important thing is that you know what your end goal is— and that is to live a more sustainable life. With that in mind, you will find that it gets easier to give up some luxuries that don't really improve your quality of life. Eventually, you will realize that the road to sustainable living is not only satisfying and fun, but it also gives you a deeper sense of purpose and meaning in your life. As you go through this borrowed time on earth, there's no greater feeling than that!

Final Words

As we have seen, you can help the world, and those actions will help you, too. The modern face of homesteading has changed over the years since the Homesteading act. Today's self-sustainable lifestyle is adaptable and achievable, no matter where you live.

We can learn much from every edge of the homesteading spectrum. If you're able to go all out with being off-grid and completely self-reliant, good for you! That is my ultimate personal goal. Even if you can't drop everything and move to the country, you can still make some lifestyle changes that can positively impact the Earth, your health, and your finances.

If this book has helped you in any way, would you please consider leaving a review where you purchased this book online? I sincerely value your feedback. Thank you in advance!

Printed in the USA
CPSIA information can be obtained
at www.ICGtesting.com
CBHW061006231024
16281CB00015B/137